Simple Jewelry

Simple Jewelry

Handcrafted designs and easy techniques

THE GUILD OF MASTER CRAFTSMAN PUBLICATIONS

First published 2016 by
Guild of Master Craftsman Publications Ltd
Castle Place, 166 High Street, Lewes,
East Sussex, BN7 1XU

Text © Clair Wolfe, 2016
Copyright in the Work © GMC Publications Ltd, 2016

All projects first published in *Making* magazine

ISBN 978-1-78494-175-8

A catalogue record for this book is available from the British Library.

Publisher: Jonathan Bailey
Production Manager: Jim Bulley
Senior Project Editor: Sara Harper
Designer: Ginny Zeal
Illustrations: Emma Cowley, Kellie Black
Photography: Step photography by Clair Wolfe; tools, equipment, and
techniques by Laurel Guilfoyle; all other photography by Emma Noren

Set in Akidenz Grotesk and Bodoni XT

Color origination by GMC Reprographics
Printed and bound in China

Contents

Introduction

This book brings together a collection of easy-to-make jewelry by accomplished designer Clair Wolfe. Jewelry making is one of the most rewarding hobbies you can have, and a fun and easy one to learn. You don't need too many expensive tools to make a start and it can be as complicated or as simple as you want it to be.

With clear text, color photographs, and detailed illustrations, most projects in the book are suitable for those new to jewelry making. There is also key information on basic materials and techniques, so that even complete beginners can tackle projects with confidence. We recommend starting with making some of the pieces exactly as they are shown to build your skill level. Then you can move on to using the projects as design inspiration rather than a set of instructions to follow, and change a few things to make the pieces your own.

Style is a personal thing, and the projects we have included will appeal to a wide range of tastes. But remember that none of these projects is set in stone. If you love blue and the project uses red then swap to blue. Or if the beads being used are too big for your liking, use smaller ones and reduce the size of the piece. You may also find you like parts of two different projects that you can mix together to produce your own unique piece.

This book is the perfect place to begin if you don't have any jewelry making experience at all. If you stick at it, you can create pieces with a real wow factor—beautiful, bespoke jewelry you can show off to your family and friends.

Tools and Equipment

The following pages explain the basic tools and equipment that you will need to make the projects in this book. Many of the miscellaneous tools are non-specialist items available in DIY and craft shops.

PLIERS AND CUTTERS

Below are the various types of pliers and cutters that you will need as a beginner. As your skills progress, there are many specialist types that are suited to particular tasks that would be a good investment.

1 Round-nose pliers

These pliers have round jaws that taper to the end and are used for making jumprings, eyepins, loops, and spirals.

2 Chain-nose pliers

These pliers have flat jaws that taper at the end. They are useful for holding small items such as neck ends and opening and closing jumprings.

3 Flat-nose pliers

These pliers have flat jaws that do not taper. They are used for holding wire, closing ribbon crimps, and opening and closing jumprings.

4 Side cutters

These cutters have the cutting jaw on the side—they have a pointed nose and can cut flush to your piece. The point also allows the cutters to access smaller areas.

5 Scissors

Small, sharp, pointed scissors are used for trimming cords, ribbon, and thread, and cutting shrink plastic.

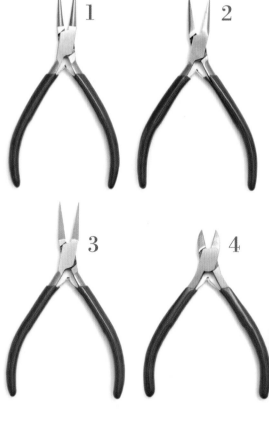

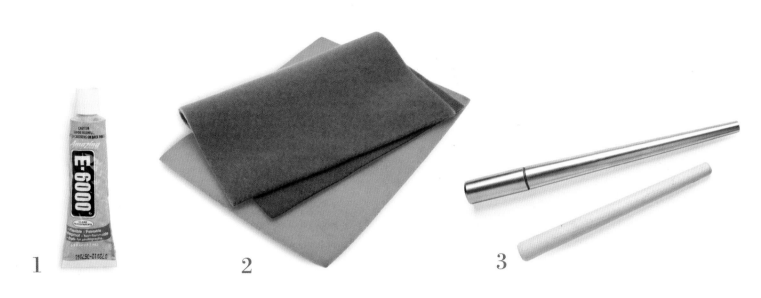

MISCELLANEOUS TOOLS

You may already have some of these useful bits of kit at home. Have a hunt around and see what you can repurpose. From a DIY hammer for flattening metal, to wooden dowels as mandrels, household items can help keep costs down when starting out.

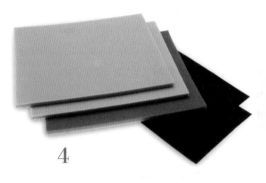

1 Adhesive

When making jewelry, use glues that are suited to the purpose. Many cyanoacrylate glues (also known as superglue) can react with metals and melt materials, though this type of glue can be used for certain tasks. White glue (PVA) is a common glue that is often used when working with children and can be used to seal paper. Liquid cement-style glue is good for adding to knots to make them extra strong. Industrial, thick, silicone-based glues, such as E6000, are used to coat wire to stop sharp edges from scratching skin and for sticking shrink plastic to combs and metal findings. **Note:** Please make sure you always use adhesives in a well-ventilated area.

2 Bead mats

These mats feel like velvet and have a texture that holds on to beads, and prevent them from rolling around on the work surface.

3 Mandrels

These are useful for making rings and bangles. They come in a variety of sizes and shapes, in both plastic and metal.

4 Emery paper

This is used to soften sharp edges on findings and wire or to smooth the edge of clay pieces. Specialist foam-backed emery paper holds its shape and works really well on clay.

5 Beading needles

Fine needles are available to use with beading thread. They come in a few different sizes and are made to go through tiny seed beads with very small holes.

FINDINGS

Findings are the items that you need to finish off your jewelry so that you can wear it. These include:

1 Clasps

There are many different types of clasp available, including slides, bolts, triggers, and even magnetic varieties. Choose a clasp to suit your design.

2 Jumprings

A jumpring is a single ring of wire that is used to join pieces together. They are available in every size you can think of and many different colors.

3 Headpins and eyepins

These are pieces of wire with a flat or ball end (headpin) or a loop at the end (eyepin). Thread a bead onto the wire and make a loop at the open end to secure the bead in place. Eyepins can be linked together to make a chain.

4 Earwires

Earwires come in various styles, from a simple "U" shape with a loop, to ones with a bead and coil finish. The loop is opened to thread on the earring piece.

5 Crimp beads and covers

Crimp beads look like small metal beads with large holes or tubes. They work by compressing stringing materials together to hold them in place. Used with crimp beads, crimp covers go over the crimp to make it look like a normal small bead. Crimp beads and covers are available in a variety of metal-color finishes.

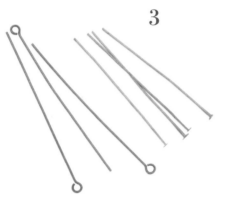

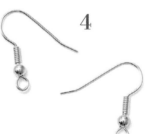

STRINGING MATERIALS, WIRE, AND CHAIN

There are many things that can be used to string your jewelry into necklaces or bracelets, including nylon-coated beading wire, beading thread, clear elastic, leather, cotton thong, and suede.

1 Nylon-coated beading wire

This wire is available in a range of brands and is really good for stringing, as it has a better strength for heavy pieces than ordinary threads. It also holds a nice shape on the neck.

2 Leather/cord/suede

These materials are available in various colors and thicknesses. They can be knotted securely with ease or used with ribbon crimps or neck ends.

3 Wire

Wire comes in a large range of sizes. It is often referred to in the USA by gauge, and in the UK by millimeters, and is also sometimes known by Standard Wire Gauge (SWG). When starting out, buy plated wire, as it is much cheaper than precious metal. Look for a non-tarnishing variety so it doesn't discolor against your skin.

4 Chain

There are many styles of chain and a variety of colors available. Fine chains are good for hanging pendants and large-link chains are good for making charm bracelets or when adding beads to the individual links.

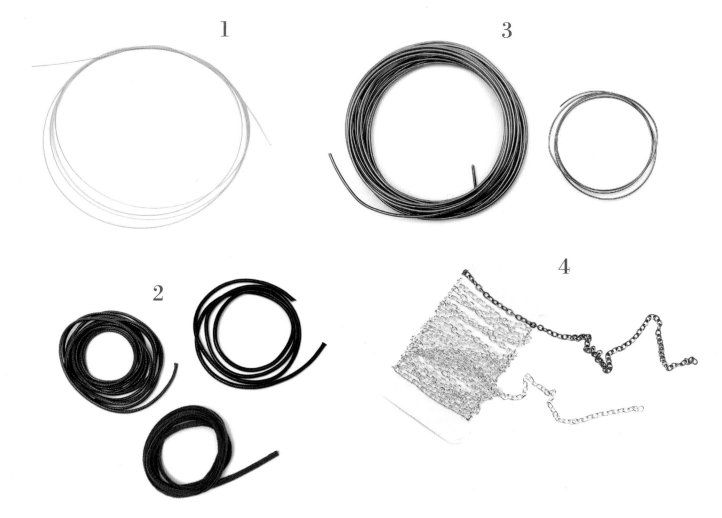

Techniques

The following pages will illustrate some of the basic techniques needed to make your own jewelry and complete the projects in this book.

Opening and closing a jumpring

To make sure that jumprings shut securely, it is important to know how to open and close them correctly. You will need two pairs of pliers with flat jaws—chain-nose or flat-nose pliers will work.

1 Take a jumpring with the opening centered at the top and hold in two pairs of pliers. Holding the jumpring this way—with one pair of pliers across one side of the ring—helps to stabilize large rings.

2 You can also hold the pliers this way, with both pairs facing inward. Both ways are fine, and the way you need to attach the jumpring often dictates how you hold it.

3 Hold the jumpring on both sides and twist one hand toward you and the other hand away. This will keep the ring round in shape. Reverse the action to close the ring. Don't ever pull the ring apart as that will warp the shape. Use this technique to open loops on eyepins, too.

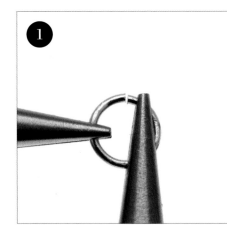

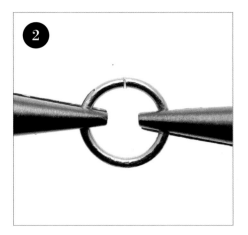

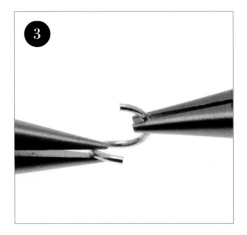

If you find that pliers mark the jumprings, wrap a bit of masking tape around the ends.

Making jumprings

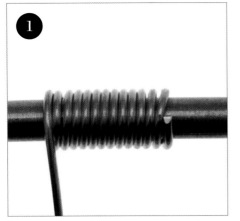

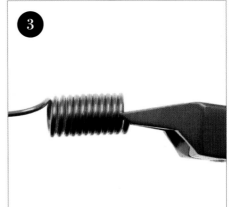

If you use a lot of jumprings and want them in different sizes, it is very easy to make them from spare ends of wire.

1 Using a rod that is the correct diameter for the jumprings you want, such as a knitting needle, wind the wire around the rod to make a coil. US 20-gauge (SWG 21, 0.8mm) wire will work well for rings under 8mm. Use larger wire for bigger jumprings. Keep the coil as tight as you can.

2 Take a pair of side cutters—if you can get semi-flush ones they will give the best result—and with the flat side facing the coil, snip off the very end.

3 Turn the cutters around so that the flat side faces away from the main coil and snip the ring off the coil. Get the pliers as close to the cut end as possible to achieve a full circle of wire.

4 When you have cut each ring off you'll see the end looks beveled, as in this image. You need to get rid of this beveled edge to give your rings a straight edge so they close well.

5 Turn the cutters again and snip off the very end of the coil (as in Step 2); do this for each ring. This feels long-winded but it makes your jumprings look better. When cut, your rings should look like this one. To close the gap on the ring, hold it in the pliers as per the instruction on the facing page and wiggle the ring back and forth, pushing the ring gently together.

Attaching a cord end

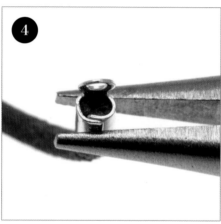

There are lots of different styles of end to choose from, so pick one to complement the piece you are making.

1 Take a cord end and place the end of the cord level with the end by the loop.

2 Press one side over the cord with chain-nose or flat-nose pliers.

3 Now press the opposite side over the top of the side that is already against the cord. Press the edge of the cord end from the middle or it will not bend level.

4 Use the pliers to make sure the tube you have created is even and the cord end looks tidy. Give the pliers a good squeeze to make sure the end is secure.

Making a wrapped loop

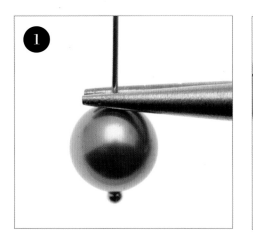

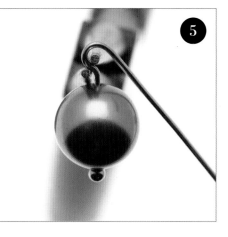

Loops have a multitude of functions in making jewelry, so this is a skill worth mastering. This style of loop is the most secure. Once attached, it cannot be removed unless it is cut off.

1 Thread a bead onto a head or eyepin. Grip the wire with round-nose pliers next to the bead.

2 Bend the wire above the plier jaw to a right angle. You will need about ⅛in (3mm) of wire above the bead before the bend.

3 Move the plier jaws to sit at the top of the bend.

4 Use your thumb to push the wire back around the pliers, keeping it tight to the jaw.

5 Keep pushing the wire around the jaw until you meet the bead.

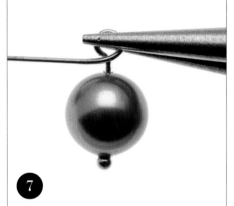

6 Move the pliers around the loop to hold it close to the open side and continue to bend the wire around until it is facing out at a right angle. You should have a complete loop.

7 If adding the loop to chain or a jumpring, thread the loop onto the chain at this stage. Use a pair of chain-nose pliers to hold the loop firmly. Make sure any chain or ring is above the pliers.

8 Wrap the wire around the neck of the loop until it meets the bead.

9 Use side cutters to snip off any excess wire. Make sure the flat side of the cutter jaws is facing the coil.

10 Take the chain-nose pliers and push the cut end of the wire into the coil, so that it sits flush.

Making a simple loop

A simple, or open, loop can be opened and closed to allow it to be attached and detached as desired.

1 Thread the bead onto a head or eyepin and cut the pin about ⅜in (10mm) above the bead.

2 Bend the wire to a right angle above the bead.

3 Using round-nose pliers, grasp the wire at the very end and curl it around the plier jaws.

4 Roll the wire around to meet the bead.

5 Move the plier jaws around the loop to sit by the bead, away from the open end. Bend the loop back to sit directly above the bead.

6 Use chain-nose pliers to tighten the loop by wiggling it until the gap is closed.

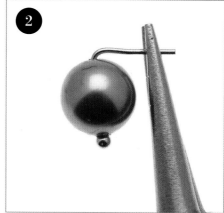

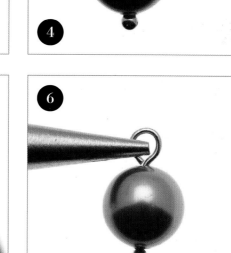

Attaching a clasp to the end of a necklace or attaching beaded pieces made on eyepins is simple and makes an attractive chain.

1 Take two pairs of chain-nose, or other flat-jaw pliers and open the loop on a beaded piece by holding the side away from the opening steady and twisting the open side toward or away from you (the same way as in the opening jumprings technique on page 12). Only open the loop as far as you need to thread on other loops.

2 Attach the next loop or a jumpring and close the loop by reversing the twist. Don't pull the loop outward or it will distort.

Make sure you close your jumprings tightly for a professional finish.

Using crimp beads

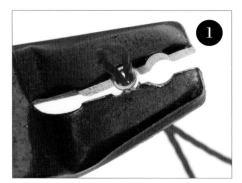

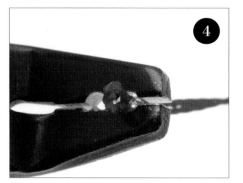

A crimp bead can be either tube-shaped or spherical—they both work the same way. If crimps are done correctly they will provide a strong hold for any type of stringing material.

1 Feed the crimp onto thread and create a loop by threading the strand back through the crimp bead. Hold the crimp bead in the pliers with the bead sat in the hole that has a round side opposite a "W" shape. The crimp should be level with the edge of the plier jaws.

2 Before closing the pliers, make sure the bead is straight, otherwise the crimp will not close correctly. Press the pliers to close the crimp.

3 Move the "U"-shaped crimp to the other hole in the pliers with two round sides. Turn the crimp so the "U" faces sideways to the plier jaws.

4 Close the pliers tightly. This will push the sides of the "U" shape together to make a tube shape again, with the thread trapped securely.

Adding a crimp cover

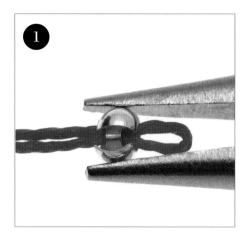

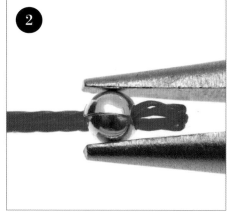

To give a professional-looking finish, it's a good idea to cover crimp beads with a crimp cover.

1 Take a crimp cover and place it over the crimped bead, making sure the bead is completely inside the cover. Take a pair of chain- or flat-nose pliers and carefully grasp the cover either side of the opening.

2 Gently press the bead closed, making sure it closes completely with the sides together.

STRINGING
and
WEAVING

Braided bracelet

———

Create chunky, easy-to-wear bracelets to match your outfit by the simple method of winding threads around chain links. Use a selection of tonal colors to add interest to the braid. Save extra threads to make tassels and matching earrings.

Materials

- Selection of embroidery threads
- Approximately 15in (38cm) length of chain, enough to fit twice around your wrist
- Findings selection (see page 10)
- Scissors
- Braiding board or similar
- Sticky tape
- Pliers
- Tape measure

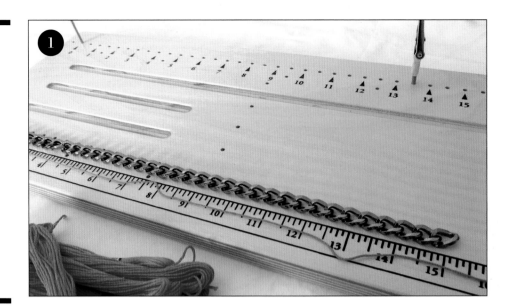

Tip
If the thread snags on the chain, gently pull back into line.

1 Unwind the embroidery thread into lengths of approximately 45in (115cm). It is better to have too much thread, as it can be snipped away easily at the end, but adding more will be tricky. You will need between 24 and 30 lengths of thread, depending on how thick you would like the braid to be. Take all the lengths of embroidery thread and use an overhand knot at one end to secure all the threads together: form a loop and pass the end through it, then tighten.

Use scissors to snip away excess threads. Divide threads into two, so you have equal numbers of threads on each side. Secure the chain on your work board; use a braiding board if you have one, but two nails tapped into a wooden board will work just as well.

2 Use small pieces of sticky tape on the ends of the thread lengths; this will keep them all together, as well as making it easier to pass them through the chain.

3 Starting at the first link, pass one cord down through the link and the second cord up through the link. Next, cross the bottom cord over the top cord, just like braiding,

4 Repeat, passing one cord from the top, and the second from the bottom.

5 Repeat the above braiding steps for the entire length of the chain. Once the end is reached, tie a second overhand knot as close to the chain as possible. Once again, use scissors to snip away excess thread. Finally, choose suitable findings for the bracelet.

6 If using toggle-style clasps, use the pliers to add them with a couple of extra jumprings (see page 12), forming a short chain, so that it is easy to do up.

Knotted necklace

_____

Throughout history gemstones have been used for their healing properties. Choose a selection of stones that you feel drawn to, and make an incredibly personal necklace using a simple knotting technique and macramé cord.

Materials

- Macramé thread
- Gemstone or pendant
- Selection of semiprecious beads
- Cutters or scissors
- Lighter
- Toothpick
- Craft glue
- Tape measure or ruler

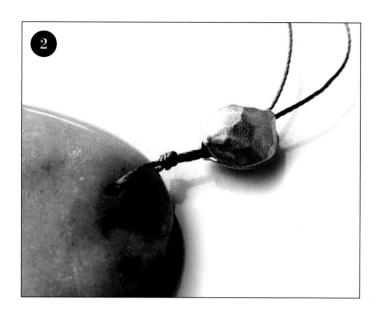

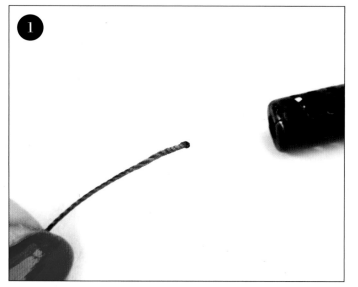

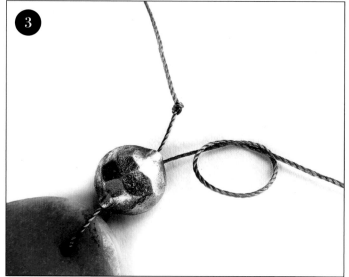

1 Cut a 1yd (90cm) length of macramé thread; this can easily be cut down later if needed. Take a lighter and run the end of the thread through the flame until it begins to melt—this will happen very quickly. While the thread is still hot, roll it between your fingers to create a stiffened end, which will be easier to pass through the gemstone or pendant and beads.

2 Pass the thread through your chosen gemstone or pendant and pull the thread until it is in the center of the thread. Use an overhand knot on the two threads and position the knot close to the top of the bead or pendant. Pass the two threads through a bead and use this bead to cover the knot.

3 Add a knot to each of the strands a short way up from the bead.

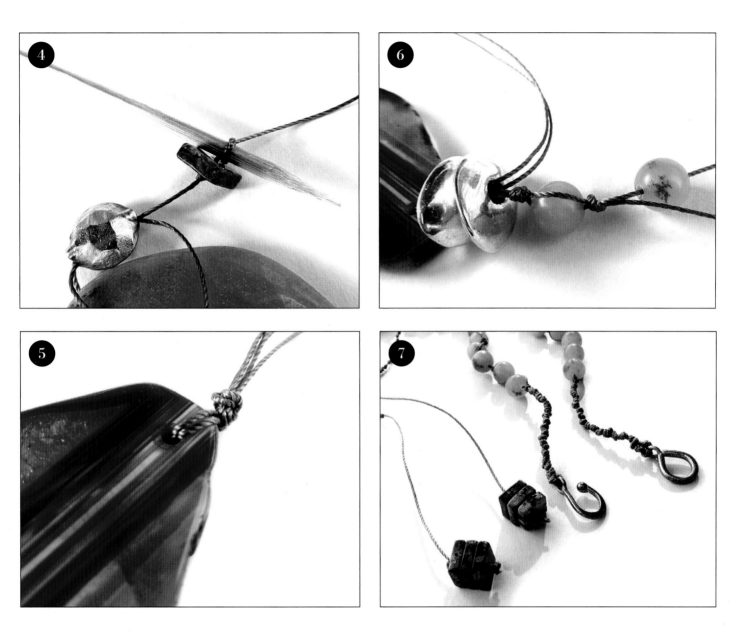

4 Thread another bead onto one of the strands and position above the knot made in Step 3. Add a knot to the top of this bead; use a toothpick or similar to help position the knot if needed. Add all the beads in this way.

5 A slight variation is to add two lengths of macramé thread. Pass the threads through the pendant and knot, as before. Add beads on all of the strands to cover the knot.

6 Add a knot to two of the strands together on one side, and repeat on the two remaining strands. Add a bead onto one of the two strands and then use both to add the knot above. Repeat with all the beads.

7 After the last bead has been added, continue to add knots along the length of the thread. To finish, add a clasp with a couple of knots and a dab of glue. Alternatively, add a small cluster of beads to each of the ends; this will allow the length of the necklace to be adjusted.

Fan bead necklaces

Make simple fan necklaces using basic stringing skills. You can buy fan bead sets in many colors and sizes. They make fabulous necklaces on their own; however, mixing two contrasting colors can lead to some really interesting and beautiful jewelry. Finish off the necklace with colorful seed beads or a chain.

Materials

- Bead and seed bead selection
- Findings selection (see page 10)
- Chain
- Beading wire
- Crimping pliers
- Flat-nose pliers
- Tape measure or ruler

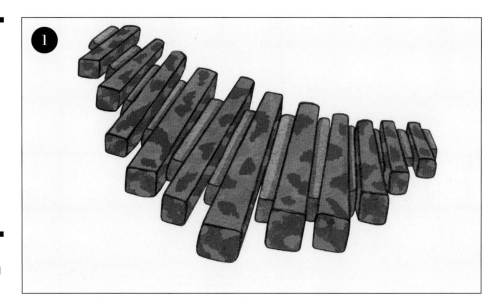

1 Take your time and have fun playing around with the beads to find a configuration that you like. Lay the beads out in the order they are to be threaded. This project shows two different designs, created using the same base skills.

2 The first design requires four equal lengths of beading wire, about 20in (50cm) long; thread the beads in the pattern order. The second design only requires one length of beading wire. Once all the beads have been threaded, double check that they are symmetrical, and correctly positioned.

3 Add a selection of seed beads to each of the four lengths of wire, on one side of the necklace. Loosely plait the four beaded wires then thread a crimp and a closed jumpring, and then pass the wire back through the crimp, leaving a loop. Secure the crimp beads with crimp covers (see page 19). Repeat on the second side.

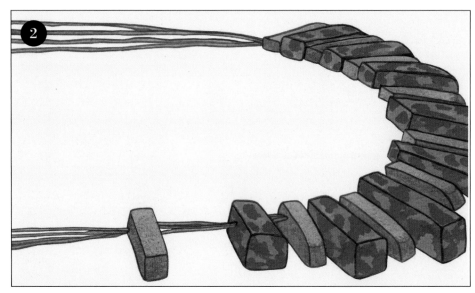

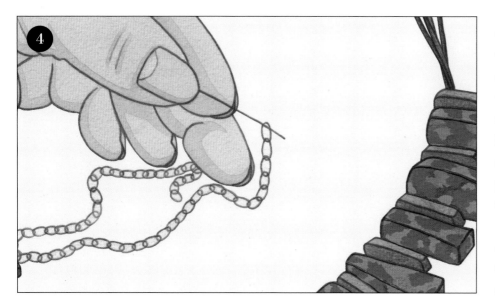

4 Use chain to finish the necklace with one strand of beading wire (the second design). Thread the beading wire through each link of the chain, until the required length of chain has been covered. Once again use crimping beads or tubes and crimping pliers to secure. Repeat on the second side of the necklace.

5 To finish both of the necklaces, snip away any excess wire left after crimping and then use suitable findings to attach the chosen clasps (see page 10).

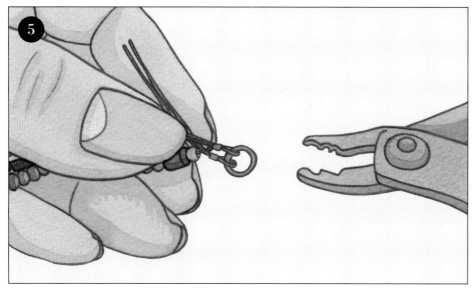

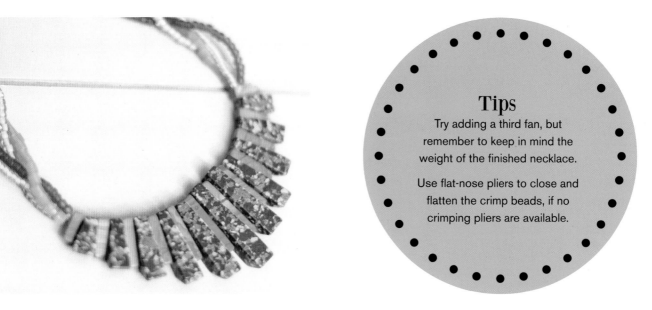

Tips

Try adding a third fan, but remember to keep in mind the weight of the finished necklace.

Use flat-nose pliers to close and flatten the crimp beads, if no crimping pliers are available.

Multi-strand bead necklace

Take simple stringing up a notch and create a colorful multi-strand necklace. For a more rustic look, swap the silver-plated beads for wooden ones, and use leftover beads to create matching earrings and a bracelet.

Materials

- Selection of colorful beads
- Selection of silver-plated beads
- 2 x silver-plated cone bead ends
- Beading board or similar
- Beading wire
- Chain
- Findings selection (see page 10)
- Crimping pliers and round-nose pliers
- Tape measure or ruler

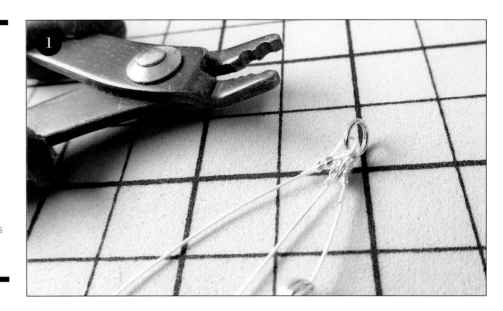

1 Cut three lengths of beading wire, approximately 16, 18, and 20in (40, 45, and 50cm). Add two crimp beads to the ends; pass the wire through a closed jumpring and then back through the crimp beads. Use crimping pliers to securely close the crimps (see page 19). Add the lengths of wire to the jumpring in size order with the shortest being positioned at the top.

2 Secure the jumpring so that it stays in place, either using a notch on a beading board, or a bulldog clip on some sturdy card. Begin to add beads to the longest wire, adding spacers as well, which will be used to connect all three strands. Once the longest strand is beaded, finish with two crimp beads and a closed jumpring (see page 12). Bead the next two strands as the first, making sure the spacers are passed through at the same point. Each strand will need fewer beads; make sure the beads sit neatly against each other as well as all having a central point. Finish with crimps.

3 Open the eye of an eyepin, add to the jumpring at the end of the beads, and then close securely. Thread the eyepin through a cone bead end.

4 Add a bead and then use round-nose pliers to make a loop. Finish the loop by coiling the excess wire (see pages 15–16).

5 Make up a selection of beads with coiled loops on both ends, and then use these to create two sections of chain. Add these to each end of the beaded section, and finish with a suitable clasp. The clasp needs to be strong and secure enough to hold the weight of all the beads included in this design.

6 If the necklace will not sit properly, use this step to make an alteration. Snip the center of the shortest wire and remove the beads until the first spacer is reached. Add a bead and a crimp and create a small loop on each side (see page 17) then add a short beaded chain section. This will save you from starting the whole necklace again.

Beaded cuff

————————

You will need a small beading loom to make this fabulous cuff, but it is very cheap, and easy to use. Either follow a pattern, or create your own unique design on graph paper using colored marker pens to show the position of each bead.

Materials

- Thick cord
- Bead selection
- Beading loom
- Beading needle and thread
- Findings selection (see page 10)
- Scissors or cutters
- Glue
- Tape measure or ruler

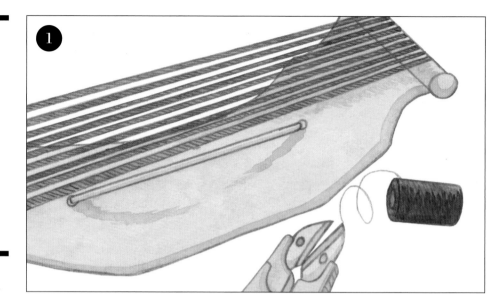

1 Follow the instructions for your particular loom. Double space the cord on the loom as each warp is added to accommodate the size of the beads being used. There needs to be an even number of warps, so that there will be an odd number of rows of beads. Once the loom is set, the tension rod can be removed.

2 Thread a beading needle with beading thread, using a manageable length. Pass the needle over the first warp, and then under the second, continuing across all the warps so that you finish going over the last warp. Return using the same process, then repeat the first pass.

3 Thread the beads onto the needle, following the pattern. Pass them along the thread and position them so that each bead slots in between two of the warps.

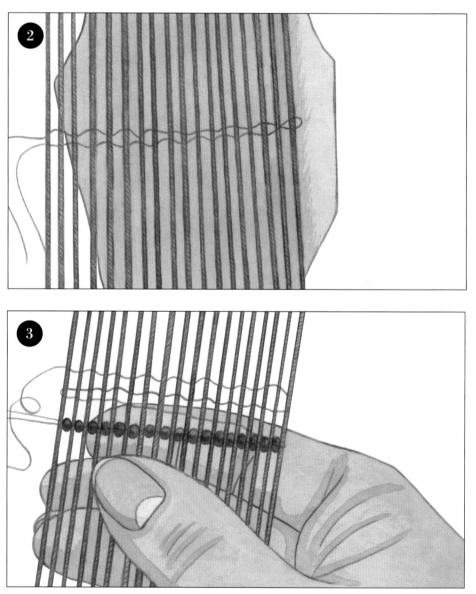

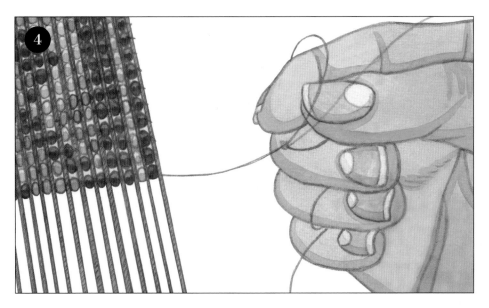

4 Hold in place by positioning a finger underneath the beads, then pass the needle back through the beads, making sure the needle and thread pass over the warp. Continue until the pattern is complete; pass any remaining thread back through the beads (this will keep all of the beads in place) and secure with a knot.

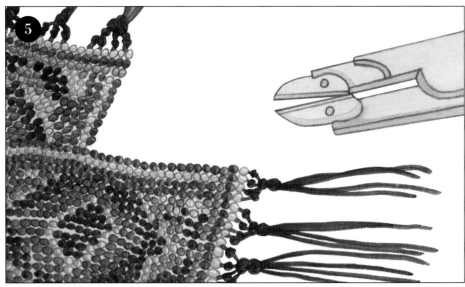

5 Carefully release the cuff from the loom, by snipping a thread at a time (the tension will cause the loom to "spring"). Take the first two threads and knot together, then do the same with all the remaining threads. Knot the central three knots, and remaining two on each side, together. Add a dab of glue to each knot.

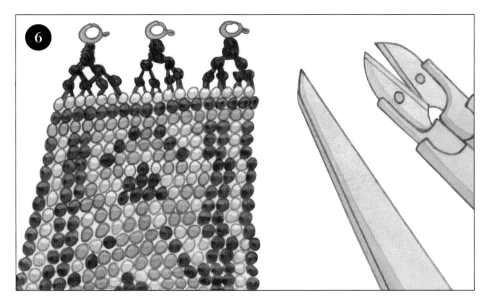

6 Take two of the central strands of beading thread, threading a closed jumpring on one (see page 12), and knot securely, once again adding a dab of glue to secure the knot. Repeat with the remaining strands, replacing jumprings with clasps on the second side. Once the glue has dried, carefully snip away loose threads.

Spiral bead necklace and earrings

Use seed beads and a simple tubular peyote stitch to create this structural cellini spiral set. It looks intricate, but it is an easy process. As you pull each different-sized bead, a delicate spiral tube will start to form.

Materials

For the Necklace

- Beading needle and thread
- Seed bead selection in sizes 6, 33mm (A); 8, 25mm (B and C); 11, 18mm (D and E); 15, 13mm (F and G)
- 2 x bead caps
- Findings selection (see page 10)
- Scissors and selection of pliers
- Glue
- Cord, ribbon, or beading wire
- Tape measure or ruler

For the Earrings

- Earring hoops
- Selection of beads
- Beading needle and thread
- Scissors
- Glue

CELLINI SPIRAL NECKLACE

1 Take a beading needle and thread it with a manageable length of color-coordinating thread. Pass the needle through the beads in the following order, two G, two F, two E, two D, two C, two A, two B, and finally two A. Leave a long tail of thread and then secure the beads into a ring, with a couple of knots and a dab of glue.

2 Pass the needle back through the first two G beads, and then add a G bead to the needle and pass it along the thread. Pass the needle through the second F bead, then add an F bead to the needle and pass it along the thread. Pass the needle through the second E bead and then add an E bead to the needle and pass it along the thread.

3 Repeat the above step through beads D, C, A, B and then A again. The needle then needs to be passed through the G bead added in the first round. This is the technique for the whole process. As you stitch the remaining rounds, always pick up the same type of bead as the bead that your thread is coming out of.

4 Hold on to the long tail of thread as you add the beads. Keeping a relatively tight tension, pull snugly on each bead as it is added. This will make the beads start to form a spiral tube. As the tube forms, you will be able to hold onto it as you add more and more rounds.

5 As you near the last 4in (10cm) of thread, remove the needle and use an overhand knot to add a new length of thread. Pull the knot as close to the last bead added as possible. Add a dab of suitable glue and then add a second knot. The glue is important to hold the knot securely in place. Allow to dry; do not trim the excess thread just yet.

6 Once you have reached the length needed for the necklace, both of the ends will need to be made slightly narrower. Continue to stitch rounds in the same way, but adding only B beads for two rounds and the D beads for another couple of rounds. To secure, pass the needle through the final round of beads a few times, pull tight and then add a knot and dab of glue.

7 Go back to each of the knots where extra thread was added; make sure each is still secure. If not, tighten, add another dab of glue and knot once again, allowing time to dry. Snip away any excess thread as close to the knot as you can without damaging it.

8 Cellini spirals can be finished by sewing on the findings, or by threading onto cord, ribbon, or beading wire. At each end add a selection of beads, a bead cap and other chosen findings.

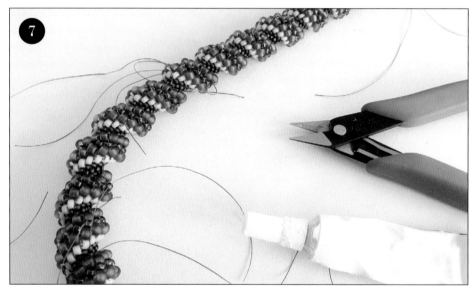

BEADED EARRINGS

1 Select a few of the beads left over from the necklace. You will need to have beads with a hole large enough to thread onto a pair of silver ear hoops. Thread five of the largest beads onto the earring hoop; there needs to be a gap big enough for the beading needle to pass through. Thread the needle with a length of thread and secure it to one side of the hoop with a couple of knots. Do not trim the thread.

2 Pass the beading needle through the first of the beads on the hoop, pick up a smaller bead and then pass the needle through the next large bead on the hoop. Continue this through all the beads.

3 Add a bead that is smaller again, this time pass the needle through the first of the second row of beads. Once again add beads of the same size along the length of the beads.

4 For the final row, add three of the smallest beads and then pass back through the first bead of the third row. Continue through all of the beads.

5 Pass the needle back through all of the largest beads; this will bring you back to the knot and the other end of the thread. Pull until all the beads are snug and then finish with a couple of knots and a dab of glue. Adjust the beads so the knot is covered. Snip the excess threads.

Wooden bead necklace

Wooden beads come in all shapes and sizes; there are numerous types of wood and many finishes. Try adding two or three different kinds of beads, all attached with good quality findings, to create a really easy and wearable necklace.

Materials

- Selection of leather cords
- Selection of wooden beads
- Cord ends
- Findings selection (see page 10)
- Beading wire
- Crimping pliers
- 2 pairs of flat-nose pliers
- Scissors
- Cutters
- Tape measure or ruler
- Glue

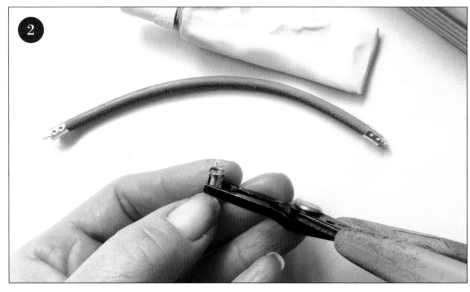

1 Measure three 8in (20cm) lengths of thick leather cord and cut with a sharp pair of scissors. Use different cord thicknesses to suit the beads used in your design.

2 Add a dab of suitable glue to the end of a piece of leather, and then position the cord end. Use flat-nose pliers to close the cord end neatly (see page 14). Repeat this on all ends of the leather cords.

3 Cut three lengths of beading wire, approximately 8, 10, and 12in (20, 25, and 30cm). Add a crimp bead and small closed jumpring to one end of each length of the wire. Thread the wire back through the crimp, and use crimping pliers to close the crimp (see page 19).

4 Thread your chosen beads onto the beading wire, until you are satisfied with the layout.

5 Add a crimp bead and closed jumpring to the other end of the wire, closing the crimp bead as close to the last wooden beads as possible. Snip away any excess wire. Repeat Steps 4 and 5 for each length of wire.

6 Attach the beaded sections to the leather sections using two pairs of flat-nose pliers and a jumpring (see page 12). Finally, add a clasp to the leather ends with two more jumprings.

Tips
Try using colorful leather for a different finish.

Add a length of chain to the clasp so the necklace length can be altered.

METAL
and
WIRE

Chain pendant

Sometimes jewelry just needs to be simple. Add a beautiful pendant to a length of fine gold chain for a simple piece of jewelry with an air of grace. Natural semiprecious stone pendants work beautifully to make a stylish set, if you wish.

Materials

- Selection of wires
- Selection of pendants
- Selection of chains
- Cutters
- 2 pairs of flat-nose pliers
- Round-nose (or looping) pliers
- Bead reamer (optional)
- Tape measure or ruler
- Superglue

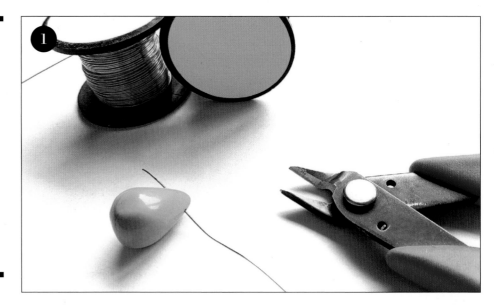

1 Use a pair of cutters to cut a length of wire approximately 3in (75cm) long (it is better to have more than you need than to try to add more wire later). The wire needs to be sturdy enough to retain its shape and hold the pendant, but narrow enough to fit through the hole in the pendant. If the hole is too small, it is possible to use a bead reamer to make it slightly larger.

2 Use either a pair of round-nose or looping pliers. Create a neat loop about a third of the way along the length of the wire and "break the neck" of the wire on both sides of the loop, so that the remaining wires line up with each other. It will look a little like a lollipop.

3 Thread the longer of the two wires through the pendant; pass it through until the looped section is just long enough to sit above the top of the pendant. Use your fingers to push the wires into position. The looped section needs to be in line with the top of the pendant.

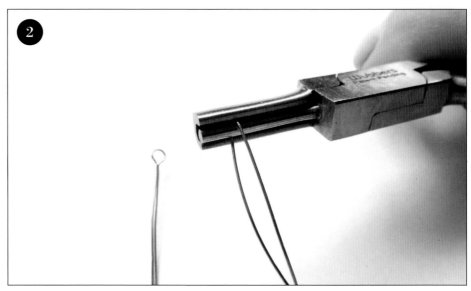

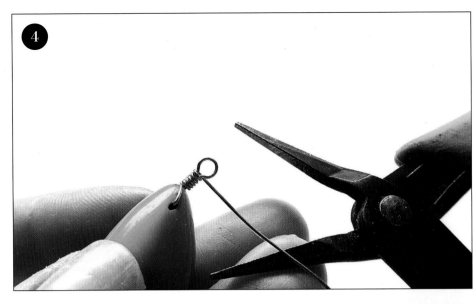

4

5

6

4 Take two pairs of flat-nose pliers, use one pair to hold the loop, then use the second pair to coil the remaining wire, working up towards the loop. Coil the remaining wire back down and over the pendant, remembering to snip away the excess wire from the loop, so it will be covered by the coils (see pages 15–16).

5 Tuck the end of the coiled wire back up inside the coil, so there will be no sharp end. Use a pair of pliers to create a right angle in the end, and then carefully push it under the coils. The next step is optional; use a dab of quick drying glue to hold everything in place.

6 Finally, add the pendant to a length of chain. Use two premade chains, removing the clasp findings, one of each, from one of the ends. Use a jumpring to add the pendant to the two loose chain ends, this will allow the pendant to hang, but not move along the chain.

Brushed brass earrings

Using a few basic hand tools and simple metal-work skills, create these tribal-inspired organic oval earrings. You can create interesting textures on the surface or give it a gently brushed look. Use beads of your choice to finish the effect.

Materials

- 0.8mm brass sheet
- US 20 gauge (SWG 21, 0.8mm) wire
- Findings selection (see page 10)
- Selection of beads
- Piercing saw
- Hammer
- Center punch
- Hand drill
- File selection
- Wire brush
- Selection of pliers
- Pencil and paper (optional)

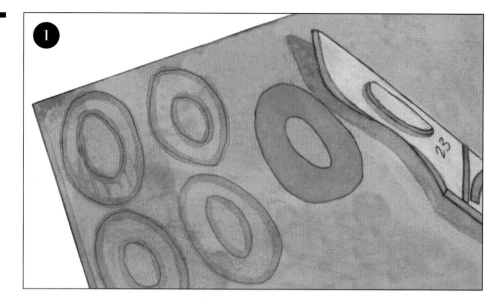

1 Create a paper pattern of an off-center oval, and then use a sharp tool to mark out the oval shape onto the protective coating or directly onto the brass sheet. Repeat until you have the required number of ovals.

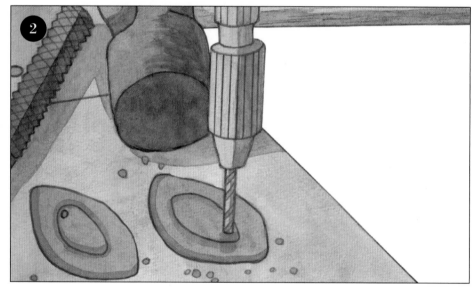

2 Using a piercing saw, follow the marked lines to cut around each of the ovals. Use a center punch and hammer just inside the inner marked oval, then use a hand drill to create a hole. Thread the blade through the hole, and carefully cut out the inner oval.

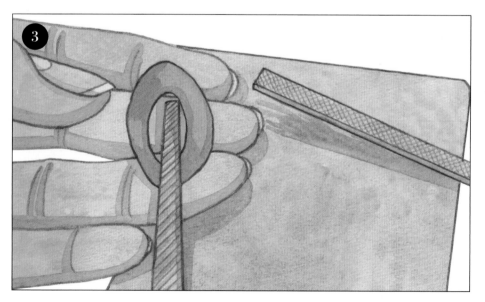

3 File to neaten the edges of the oval, using a curved file for the inner oval. Next use a hammer (an old hammer face will impart a subtle texture) and work over the entire surface; repeat on the reverse side. This will soften and gently bevel the edges as well as leaving a texture.

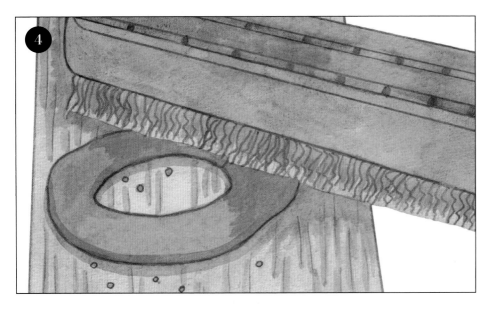

4 Place the oval onto a suitable surface and then use a wire brush over the whole surface, including the reverse side. The wire brush will give a soft brushed look to the brass. Try brushing in different directions for a really lovely finish.

5 Decide where the holes need to be in the ovals, portrait or landscape, to allow beads and earwires to be attached. Use a center punch and hammer to create a guide hole, followed with a hand drill to complete the hole. Neaten the hole with a file if needed.

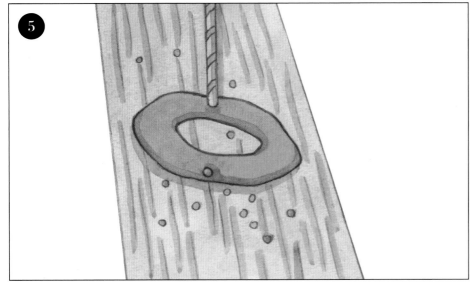

6 Lay out the ovals and position your chosen beads accordingly; the beads need to be threaded onto wire, and have loops made at each end (see page 15). Assemble all pieces by using two pairs of pliers to open and close the jumprings (see page 12). Finally, add the earwires.

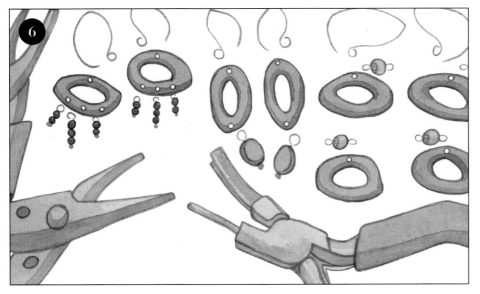

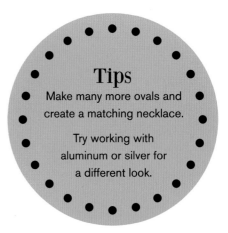

Tips

Make many more ovals and create a matching necklace.

Try working with aluminum or silver for a different look.

Crystal brooch

Create this glamorous 1950s-style brooch with a few simple tools and basic skills. It has a delicate snowflake base and is decorated with Swarovski crystals. The sparking button in the center makes this an outstanding piece of jewelry.

Materials

- 3 x snowflake wire bases
- White seed beads
- Selection of Swarovski crystals
- Sparkling button
- Needle and beading thread
- Brooch back finding
- Round-nose pliers
- Flat-nose pliers
- Glue (optional)

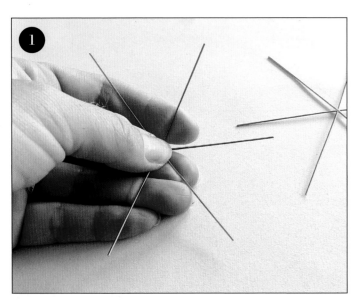

1 Place your thumb in the center of a snowflake base and gently bend the wires up, one at a time. Try not to bend at the joint, as this may snap the wire. Bend all of the wires in the same way; there only needs to be a slight bend.

2 Add beads to the first spoke on the snowflake, using plain white seed beads where they will be covered by the button. Leave about ¼in (6mm) of wire visible at the tip.

3 Use a pair of round-nose pliers to create a small loop (see page 17) in the wire, taking care not to damage the crystals. The wire used to make these forms is a version of memory wire, and therefore very stiff.

4 Use a pair of flat-nose pliers to squeeze the loop together. This is tricky and will take a little patience. Repeat the previous steps on all of the spokes, matching the bead order on opposite spokes. Make two more snowflakes in the same way.

5 Place one of the snowflakes on top of another, turning the top one around until you are happy with the layout. Thread a beading needle with a length of a good quality beading thread, doubling it over and knotting the two ends together. Sew the two flakes together, passing the needle as close to the center of the flakes as possible.

6 Place the third snowflake on top of the first two, and sew it on in the same way. Once all are secured together, turn over to the back and secure with a number of knots. Do not cut the thread.

7 Position the button and use the needle and thread to sew this in the center of the snowflakes. Add enough stitches so that the button is securely fastened. Add a brooch back finding in the same way to the back of the brooch. Finish with a few knots and a dab of glue, if desired.

Silver chain earrings

_____

Simple silver earrings make a great gift for a special occasion, adding a little festive sparkle to any outfit for the party season. Copper or brass would also work well for this design, which is flexible and allows a variety of finishes.

Materials

- 0.5mm silver sheet
- Silver chain
- Jumprings
- Findings selection (see page 10)
- Shears or sharp scissors
- Ruler
- Scribe
- Needle file
- Steel block
- Ball pein hammer
- Hammer
- Center punch
- 2 pairs of needle or flat-nose pliers
- Wire brush

1 Take a sheet of silver and mark out two triangles using a ruler and scribe.

2 Use shears or even a sharp pair of scissors to cut the triangles, taking care not to cut yourself on the sharp corners of the metal.

3 Add texture over the surface of the triangles with a small ball pein hammer; this will flatten the triangles as well as giving them strength.

4 Using the ruler and scribe once more mark out points on the back of the triangle where holes will be added.

5 Place the triangle on a steel block; use a center punch and hammer to create the holes using the marks as a guide. Neaten holes with a needle file.

6 Use two pairs of needle or flat-nose pliers to open jumprings with a slight twisting motion (see page 12), add with a length of chain to the triangle, and twist back to close. Repeat for the rest of the holes. Add earring findings in the same way.

ALTERNATIVE VERSION

Follow Steps 1 and 2, and in Step 3 use a wire brush to give a satin finish. In Step 4 just mark the three corners. In Step 5 add a hole to each of the corners on the triangle. Finally, in Step 6 add the earring finding with two jumprings, and then add two lengths of chain so that they hang from the remaining triangle corners (see main project image on page 66).

Tip
Try cutting out other simple shapes from the silver sheet and making more earrings.

Charm bracelet

———————

Make good use of all the little coins collected from your vacations in other countries with this keepsake charm bracelet. Choose a selection of suitable coins; small to mid-size ones will work best for this style of bracelet.

Materials

- Coin selection
- Bracelet chain
- Sturdy jumprings
- Emery paper or polishing pad
- Renaissance wax
- Steel block
- Hand drill
- Center punch
- Hammer
- Two pairs of flat-nose pliers

1 Use a very fine grade of emery paper, or a polishing pad, to clean away grime from the coins. This will highlight the raised pattern of the coins, but leave some patina behind. Use renaissance wax to leave a protective coating on the coin.

2 Place a coin onto a steel block (or other suitable surface) and position the center punch approximately ⅛in (3mm) in from the edge of the coin. Hold steady and strike firmly with a hammer. Some coins are stamped upside down on the opposite side, so you may have to choose the hole position carefully. Use a hand drill to create the hole in each coin.

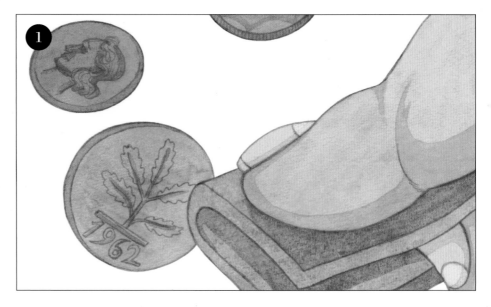

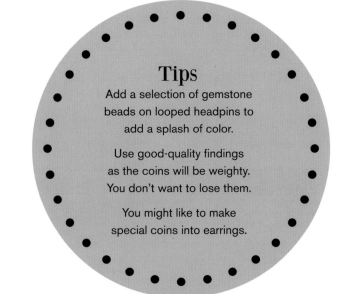

Tips

Add a selection of gemstone beads on looped headpins to add a splash of color.

Use good-quality findings as the coins will be weighty. You don't want to lose them.

You might like to make special coins into earrings.

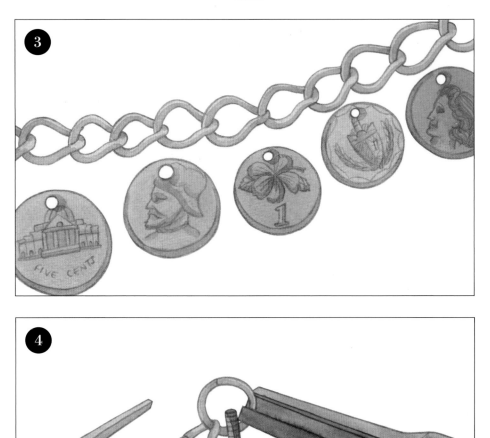

3 Once all the coins have had a hole drilled in them, lay them out in a line along the length of the bracelet chain; use a tone of bracelet metal that will blend well with the coin selection. Move the coins about until happy with their position; try to mix up the coins, so that you have a nice blend of silver, brass, and copper-colored coins along the bracelet length.

4 Finally, use really good quality, sturdy jumprings to add each coin to a link on the bracelet. This is best done by using two flat-nose pliers, and twisting the jumpring open just enough to thread on the coin and attach it onto the bracelet. Close each jumpring by twisting back and forth until both ends are lined up perfectly (see page 12).

Silver and bead necklace

Use vibrant and colorful matching pairs of beads to create this necklace with a hint of textured silver. It is easily completed with basic tools and simple jewelry-making skills. You could use leftover silver sheet to make matching earrings.

Materials

- 0.3mm silver sheet
- Beading wire (soft flex)
- Findings selection (see page 10)
- Selection of beads
- Pendant
- Chain
- Emery paper
- Scissors or cutters
- Household hammer
- Center punch
- Selection of pliers
- Pencil and paper
- Round file (optional)

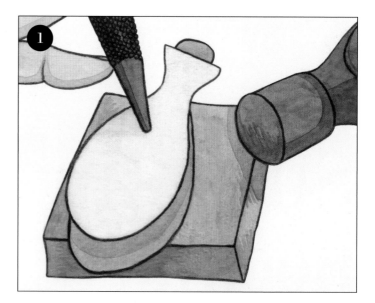

1 Work out your design with a pencil and paper, using the pendant to draw around, so that you can work out the size of the silver needed. Remember to mark the position of the pendant hole, as this will be needed later. Once happy with the design, place the paper onto the silver, and use a sharp tool to score through onto the protective plastic sheet. Use a good pair of scissors or cutters and cut out the design as carefully and neatly as possible. Take care as the silver is very thin; it will curl up and have sharp edges. Once cut out, use emery paper to remove any rough edges and burrs. Once all the edges have been smoothed over, use a center punch to add a hole. Use a round file to neaten the hole, if needed.

2 Use a hammer to work over the surface of the silver design. This will harden the silver as well as creating a gentle texture. Any household hammer will do this job. Strike the metal evenly, working over the whole surface.

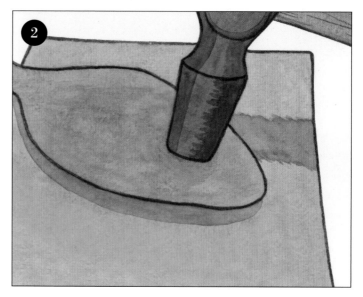

3 Place the pendant onto the silver, carefully folding the top part over. Remove the pendant, turn the silver over, and place onto a suitable surface, using the first hole as a guide to create a second hole.

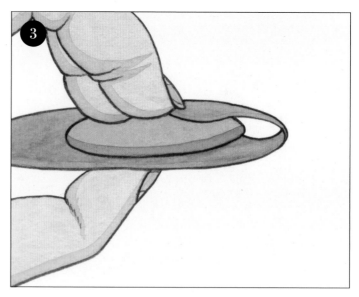

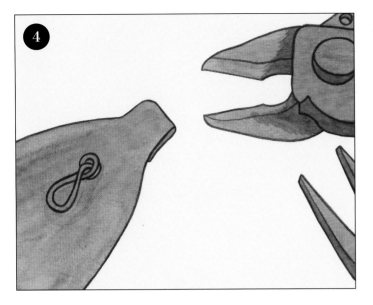

4 Place the pendant back in, lining up the holes, and pass a headpin through all three holes. Use round-nose pliers to create a loop, snip away the excess wire and flatten the loop against the silver.

5 Take a length of beading wire suitable for the weight of beads being used. Semiprecious and coral beads tend not to be uniform either in size, shape, or pattern. Sort through the beads and try to select pairs that are a similar size, shape, and color. Thread the beads onto the wire, on either side of the pendant, creating a symmetrical beaded pattern. Keep beading until the desired length is reached.

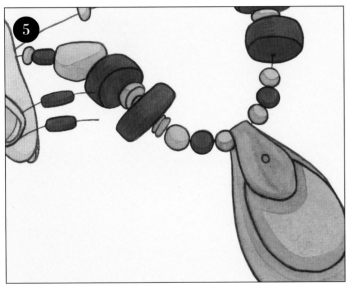

6 Finish each of the ends with a foldover cap (these are designed for cord or leather, but work well with weighty necklaces). Place the wire into the cap, pass it around the loop, then back through the cap, hold the wire in place and use pliers to fold one side over tightly, followed by the second. Snip away excess wire as close to the cap as possible. Add a chain and a clasp to finish.

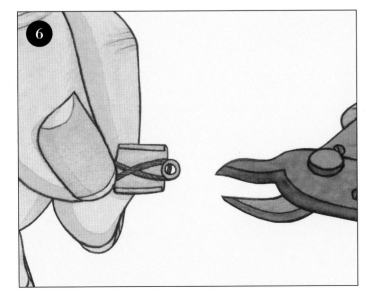

Tips
Substitute the silver sheet with copper, brass, or aluminum.

Use a good-quality, strong beading wire when using heavy beads.

CLAYS,
SILICONE,
and RESIN

Polymer clay and bead necklace

Create this vintage-inspired rose necklace with a few basic jewelry-making skills. This is a ideal opportunity to make a delicate rose in exactly the shade you prefer. It is a real statement piece with a beaded chain and hanging embellishments.

Materials

- Polymer clay
- Selection of beads
- Findings selection (see page 10)
- Acrylic roller
- Domestic oven
- Parchment paper
- Scissors
- Round-nose pliers
- 2 pairs of flat-nose pliers
- Cutters
- Emery paper
- Polymer glaze (optional)
- Craft glue (if needed)

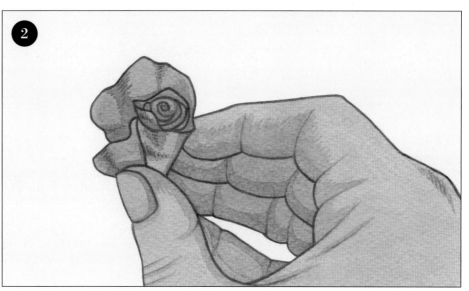

1 Polymer clay, like paint, can be mixed and blended to make any color needed in a project, which is ideal when you can't find the exact color you want. Follow the clay instructions to prep the clay, and then mix the colors until you are happy with the shade. Take care not to add air to the clay as it can become trapped and cause bubbles (parchment paper will protect the work surface). Once clay has been prepared, divide into small balls.

2 Flatten the clay balls between fingers and thumb to create the petals. Start the rose by taking the first petal and rolling it from one side across to the other, like rolling a rug. Wrap subsequent petals around the first and continue until the rose has been formed. Use your fingers to shape the petal edges.

Tips

Use a polymer glaze or antiquing solution on the rose for different finishes.

Use craft glue for the eyepins on the back of the rose if baking has not secured them.

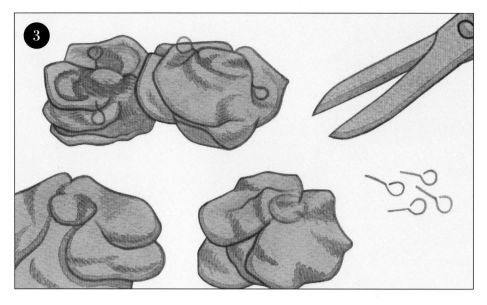

3 Use a pair of scissors to snip the excess clay from the back of the rose, push in two eyepins, and neaten the back so that it is flat and even. Take care not to damage the front of the rose. Next, use fingertips to gently manipulate each petal into the desired position. Cure the clay in a domestic oven following the manufacturer's instructions. Allow the polymer clay rose to cool completely.

4 Place a bead onto an eyepin and create a second eye with round-nose pliers, trimming away excess wire with cutters. There is no need to coil the excess wire into a loop as the eye needs to be opened and closed. Repeat until you have enough to make the length of chain needed. Connect the beads by opening the eye, adding a closed jumpring and then closing the eye neatly and securely.

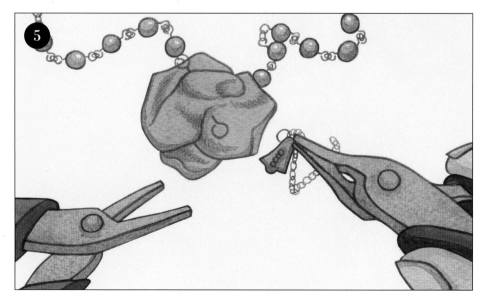

5 Using two pairs of flat-nose pliers, use open jumprings (see page 12) to add the beaded chain to the rose. Jumprings should be opened with a small twisting motion and not pulled apart, as they will be easier to close and retain their strength. Use further jumprings to add the remaining findings, including short lengths of chain and the clasp, and finally a length of chain with two beads on headpins, to the remaining eyepin on the rose.

Resin pendants

Stamps from around the globe are full of beautiful images and glorious colors. Postcards sent from distant lands with beautiful stamps are perfect to use to make these simple pendants. Here are two ways to capture the stamp and the memory forever to create treasured keepsakes.

Materials

- Stamp selection
- Picture-frame pendants
- Glass cabochons
- Findings selection (see page 10)
- Chain
- Craft glue (clear drying)
- Pencil
- Scissors
- Needle-nose tweezers
- Clean cloth
- Epoxy resin (gel)
- Craft knife

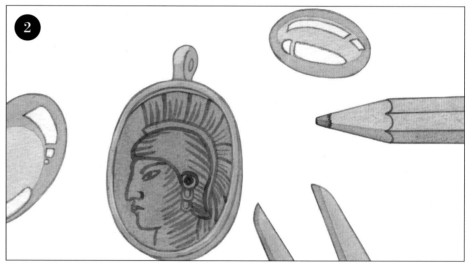

Tip

Use needle-nose tweezers to remove the stamp from the frame during the fitting process.

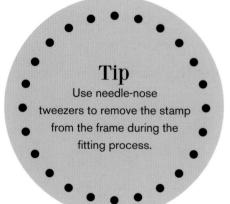

METHOD 1

1 Choose a stamp that is a suitable size for your picture-frame pendant. Use the glass cabochon, which fits inside the frame, as a template guide. Place it onto the stamp and move it around until you are happy with the picture position beneath. Use a pencil to draw around the cabochon.

2 Use a good pair of scissors to cut out the marked shape. Check it fits into the picture-frame pendant, trimming away excess if needed. Once the stamp fits comfortably into the frame, it is ready to be glued.

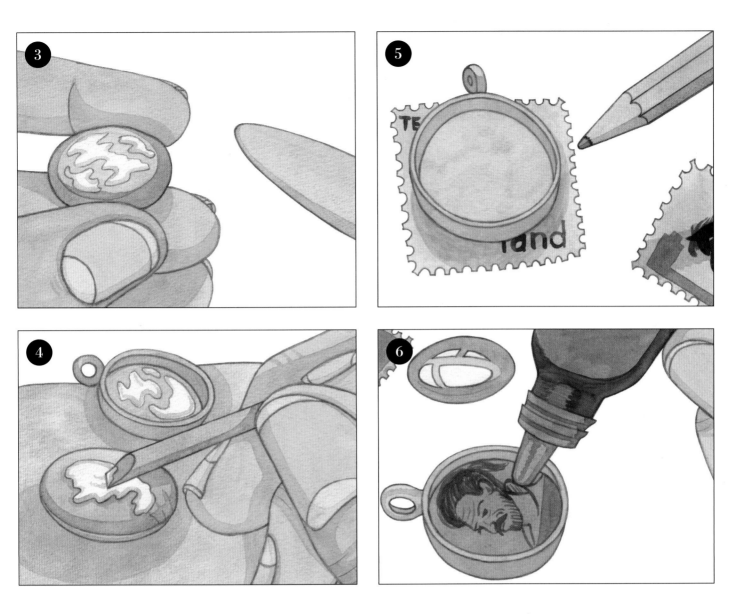

3 Add a thin layer of glue to the flat surface of the glass cabochon. Place the stamp onto the cabochon, and move around until happy with the position. Place the cabochon face down onto a non-scratch surface and use a clean cloth to gently burnish the back of the stamp. This will create a good bond, and remove excess glue and any air bubbles.

4 The next step is to add glue to the back of the stamp and to the inside of the picture-frame pendant. Leave for a moment, to allow it to become tacky, and place the cabochon into the picture frame. Remove any excess glue from the frame, and then allow to dry for several hours. Once completely dry, add to your chosen chain.

METHOD 2

1 Choose a suitable stamp, this time using the picture-frame pendant as the template (*image 5*). Draw around with a pencil and then cut out with scissors. Trim carefully until the stamp fits into the frame perfectly. The better the fit at this point the nicer the finish.

2 Gently squeeze the bottle of resin, allowing the gel to come out slowly. Add enough gel to cover the stamp and pendant surface evenly. Allow the gel to move around the pendant, making sure it touches all the walls (*image 6*). Place in direct sunlight and allow to cure. This process can be repeated until you are happy with the thickness of the resin. Add your chosen chain.

Silicone resin pendant

Create molds and then replicate a seashell with a two-part resin to form this quirky little pendant. Choose the color to match your mood, or paint the resin seashell with silver or gold to form a very special piece.

Materials

- Polymer clay and release agent
- Silicone mold resin and curing agent
- Seashells
- Findings selection (see page 10)
- Beading wire or cord (optional)
- Chain
- Hand drill
- Craft knife
- Small plastic pots
- Paint
- Paintbrush or sponge
- Kitchen scales (if available)
- Two pairs of flat-nose pliers

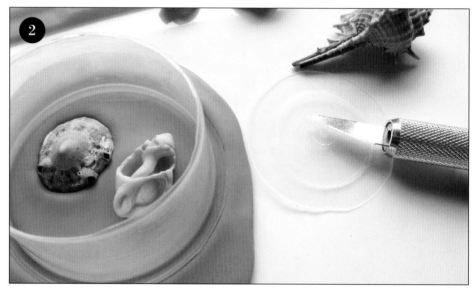

1 The first step is to construct a mold box; this can be achieved easily with small plastic pots. Use a craft knife to remove the base of the pot. Limit the amount of clay used by ensuring the pot is only a little larger than the item to be molded. Condition and roll out a the polymer clay larger than the mouth of the pot.

2 Place the pot onto the clay and push down firmly to ensure a seal is created so the rubber will not run out once it is poured into the pot. Position the shell in the pot; once again, apply pressure to ensure the shell is secured in place. Depending on the size of the shell, you may be able to position two or more shells within the pot. Use the release agent, taking care as it is a strong chemical.

3 Following the instructions, mix the stated ratio of the silicone mold resin and curing agent in a plastic pot and stir thoroughly until it is one solid color. Gently pour into the pot, ensuring it is at least ½in (1.25cm) deep over the highest point of the shell. Tap on the top of the pot to help release any air bubbles that may be trapped in the rubber. Leave the rubber to cure for the suggested time.

Hold the plastic pot and gently start to move it, releasing the pot and rubber from the clay. Once removed from the clay, remove the plastic pot and then the shell. If the shell is a complicated shape, manipulate the resin mold a little to release the shell. Finally, if needed, clear any remaining clay and debris from the mold. The mold is now ready to be used.

Once again, follow the instructions to mix the resin. Use kitchen scales for accurate measurements, if available. Once the two parts have been added to each other, there is a limited time in which to mix and pour the resin before it begins to cure. Pour into each mold, trying not to over-fill, although the excess can be easily removed once cured. Tap each mold to release any trapped air bubbles.

4 Once cured, manipulate the mold to release the resin shell. The shell can now be easily drilled; a hand drill will work best. The shell can be painted with a suitable paint, or left natural. Finally, add a jumpring using two pairs of flat-nose pliers (see page 12) and thread onto a chain. Alternatively, drill across the shell and thread onto beading wire, or cord.

Tips

Use silver paint for a silver-clay look at a fraction of the cost.

Cast lots of resin shells and create a beautiful statement necklace.

Try casting other small objects to use in your jewelry creations.

Epoxy clay
fan pendant

———————

Use two-part epoxy clay, peel-offs, and pigment ink to create this lightweight, eye-catching pendant. Choose a design that suits you or simply apply one of the wide variety of looks and finishes available to create a very unique pendant.

Materials

- Two-part epoxy clay
- Peel-off selection
- Findings selection (see page 10)
- Pigment ink
- Paint
- Craft knife
- Olive oil
- Spacers
- Tweezers
- Sponge applicator
- Cotton-wool pad
- Sanding pad
- Craft knife
- Acrylic roller
- Hand drill

1 Following the instructions on the packet, take equal quantities of both parts of epoxy clay, and mix together until the clay is uniformly colored (to create a bright white finish). The clay needs to be left to rest for approximately 15–20 minutes until has hardened as a polymer, ready to use. Once ready it has a 2–3 hour working time; plenty of time to create the pendant.

2 Rub a little olive oil on to your hands; this will prevent the clay from sticking. Wet the work surface and acrylic roller with a little water, which will help the clay to roll out easily. Place the clay onto the wet work surface between two spacers; use the acrylic roller to roll out the clay into a sheet large enough for the chosen peel-off.

3 Use fingernails or a pair of tweezers to carefully remove the peel-off from its backing sheet; try not to stretch or distort it. Allow the peel-off a few moments to return to shape before positioning it on the clay. Use the acrylic roller over the surface to ensure a good bond between the peel-off and the clay.

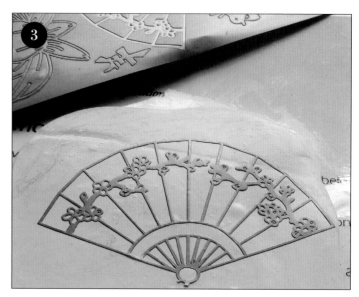

4 Use a pigment ink on the surface of the clay; dab gently using the sponge applicator. Allow to dry and apply a second coat. Once dry, use a cotton-wool pad to rub over the surface, which will remove the majority of ink from the peel-off, allowing it to shine through. Allow the clay to rest for about 30 minutes; it will begin to cure and stiffen.

5 Use a craft knife to cut around the peel-off. Make small cuts along the edge of the fan, trying not to drag the clay by cutting in one go. Don't try to remove the clay from the worksheet, but allow to cure fully. Create a curve on the fan by positioning the worksheet in a curved position between two weighty objects.

6 Once cured, remove from the worksheet and use a sanding pad to smooth the edges of the fan; emery paper or a metal file may be used if a larger area of excess needs to be removed. Paint the back and edges of the fan with a suitable paint. Use a hand drill to create holes at the top and the bottom of the fan. Finally, add your chosen findings to complete the pendant.

Tips

Create a perfectly coordinating bead by painting with the same paint and finishing with the pigment ink.

Make two smaller fans to create a matching pair of earrings.

Try using different-color clays and inks for completely different finished looks.

Bead and resin necklace

Don't throw away broken jewelry; cherished pieces can be remodeled into something new to be treasured all over again. This idea reuses a green bead necklace and combines it with a resin-filled pendant to make a stylish new piece at very little cost!

Materials

- Jewelry that can be taken apart
- Eyepins
- Findings selection (see page 10)
- Extender chain and clasp if needed
- Mild detergent
- White vinegar
- Epoxy resin
- Colored paper for background
- Round-nose pliers
- Two pairs of flat-nose pliers
- Cutters

1 Snip away the clasp and slide off the beads into a pot or a tin, to keep them all together. Depending on the age of the jewelry being taken apart, it may need to be cleaned. Make up a solution of mild detergent, white vinegar, and water, and wash and dry each bead separately; do not let them soak if you are unsure what they are made from.

2 Slide each bead onto an eyepin. Use round-nose or looping pliers to create a second loop, snipping away any excess wire with the cutters.

3 Open the loop with two pairs of flat-nose pliers, using a twisting motion, and add a closed jumpring. Reclose the loop by twisting it back into position. Repeat until the necklace is the required length, adding an extender chain and clasp if needed.

4 Have a play around with colored backgrounds: create your own using a suitable ink-based pen or ink pad, or you could use images from a magazine or use colored paper.

5 Cut the background to size and place into the pendant base, pushing right into edges and corners.

6 Follow the mixing instructions of the epoxy resin. The one used here takes two parts base to one part hardener; you will only need to mix a very small amount. Mix thoroughly, trying not to create any bubbles in the mix. Gently pour a layer of resin into the pendant base, and tilt the base to make sure the resin covers the surface. Allow to cure.

7 Once cured, mix another batch of resin as before, and add another layer. Allow this to cure, and then, if needed add a third layer of resin to create a slight domed effect. Leave to cure thoroughly in a dust-free environment; a food cover or a plastic bowl work well to prevent dust. Take the beaded necklace made in the first steps. Open up the looped beads opposite the clasp and add a closed jumpring to each of the looped beads (see page 12). Connect the two closed jumprings with a large jumpring, onto which another looped bead has been added. Add one further large jumpring and the pendant to finish.

LEATHER

Leather cuff

In a few simple steps, you can create this pretty cuff, with a selection of colorful ribbons. Embellish with seed beads to give the cuff a little sparkle and complement the color of the ribbons. For a different look you could use denim or materials other than leather—the result will be just as effective.

Materials

- Offcut leather
- Latex adhesive
- Craft glue
- Ruler
- Marker pen
- Ribbon selection
- Seed bead selection
- Embellishment selection
- Revolving leather punch
- Flathead screwdriver
- Beading needle and thread
- Scissors
- Craft knife
- Stud and screw fixings

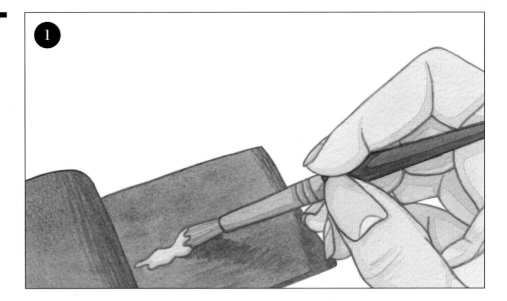

1 Use a ruler and marker pen to mark out the two sections for the cuff base. Using a craft knife or scissors, cut out the matching sections of leather. Then use a latex adhesive to stick the back sides of both pieces together. Latex adhesive dries and bonds very quickly so it's best to start at one end and work across the leather in small areas.

2 Choose a selection of ribbons; try to pick ones that will complement each other, but do not necessarily have matching colors and patterns. Try to choose differing widths and finishes and have fun experimenting. Use a beading needle and thread to add a variety of seed beads to the ribbons if desired. These will add interest and a little sparkle to the cuff.

Tips

Try replacing the leather with denim which will work well with this design.

Make lots of skinny cuffs, and wear them stacked together.

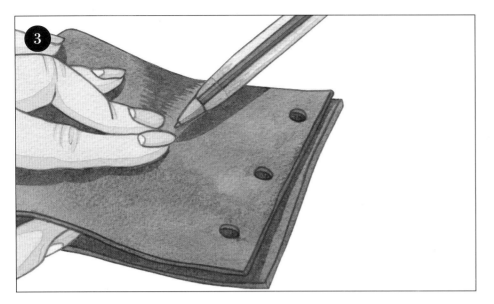

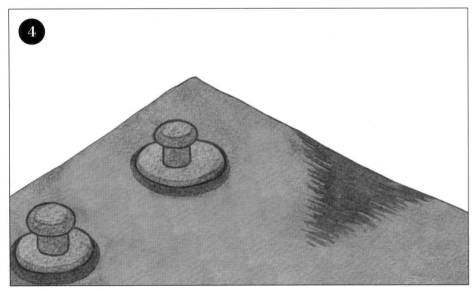

3 Use a ruler to mark equally spaced points where the holes will be made. Using a revolving leather punch, revolve until it is positioned on a suitably sized die, then punch out the holes. Use these holes to mark the position of the corresponding points on the opposite cuff end. Revolve to a larger punch and repeat.

4 Push a screw fitting through one of the holes, and then screw on the top section of the stud. Use a flathead screwdriver to tighten if needed. Repeat in each of the holes. Push the studs into the larger holes, making sure that the studs fit. They may be a little stiff and need to be "worked," but they need to be snug to keep the cuff safely on.

5 Lay the cuff flat and experiment with the layout of the ribbons until you're happy with the design. Use craft glue to stick each ribbon to the leather cuff. Glue on further embellishments. Close the cuff with the studs and allow to dry. Undo and redo the cuff a couple of times to see if there are any areas which need extra gluing. Once it is completely dry, check the cuff over for any loose threads, and snip away.

Rose quartz necklace

Rose quartz has to be one of nature's prettiest semiprecious stones, with its soft pink color and wonderful healing properties. Combined with Sterling silver and supple leather, it creates a naturally beautiful necklace.

Materials

- Selection of rose quartz beads
- US 18 gauge (SWG 19, 1mm)
  silver wire
- Leather cord
- Round-nose pliers
- Needle-nose pliers
- Shears
- Cutters
- Ruler
- Glue

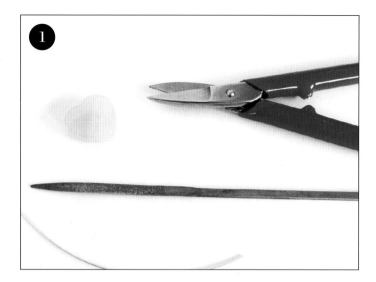

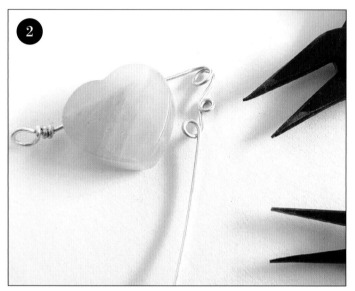

1 Choose a bead to be the focal of the necklace and then use shears or cutters to cut a length of the silver wire. The wire needs to be approximately seven times the length of the bead. Neaten both ends of the wire with a file.

2 Create a loop in the wire roughly 1in (25cm) from the end using round-nose pliers and then wrap the remaining wire to form a coil. Thread the bead onto the wire and use the round-nose pliers to form loops in the remaining length of wire, leaving a short length of unshaped wire at the end.

3 Carefully bend the shaped wire over the stone and then manipulate it with your fingers until you are happy with its placement. Use needle-nose pliers to wrap the unshaped wire around the coil from the previous step.

4 Repeat the above steps on six chunky rose quartz beads—have fun working the silver wire into different shapes.

5 Take approximately 40in (1m) length of leather and soften it with your hands. Thread the wrapped focal bead to the center of the leather and secure with a knot.

6 Thread one of the wire-wrapped beads onto one side of the leather cord and secure in place with a knot. Add a bead to the other side of the cord, level with the first bead. Secure into position with a knot.

7 Repeat the above step with the remaining beads. Positioning the beads symmetrically like this will help the necklace to sit nicely when being worn. There are various ways to finish the necklace, but a noose knot will allow the necklace length to be adjusted according to the outfit being worn.

8 Cut an 8in (20cm) length of leather and add five or six loose coils over the two necklace cords. Pass one of the ends back through the coils and then do the same with the other side. Pull both ends to tighten the leather coils. Add knots to each of the cords as close to the coils as you can. Add knots to the ends of the necklace cords and finish each knot with a dab of glue.

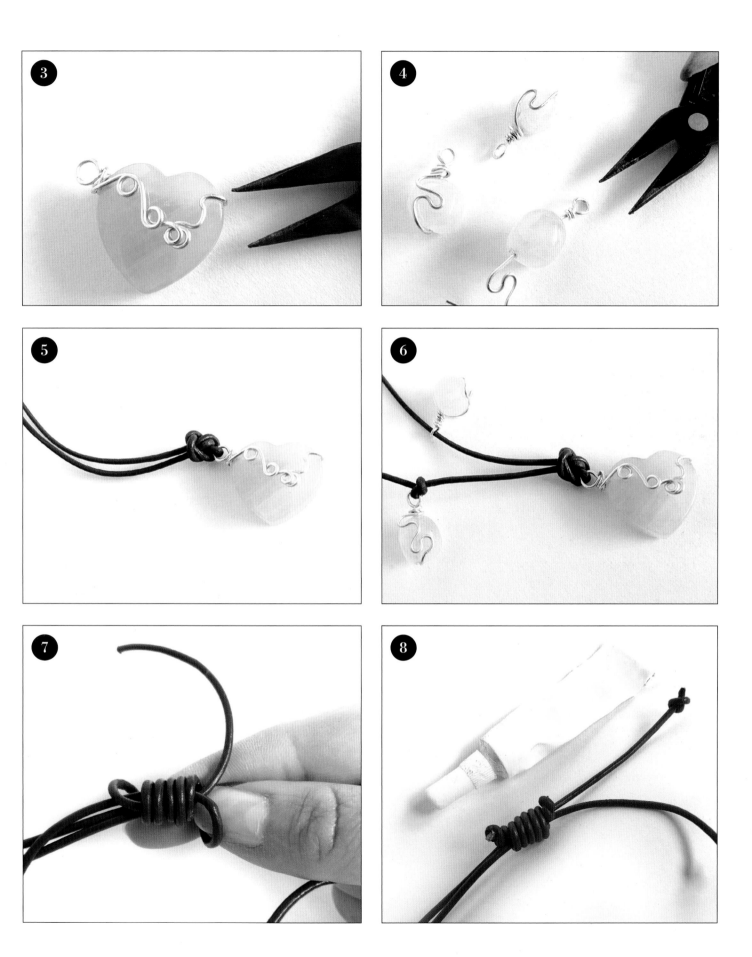

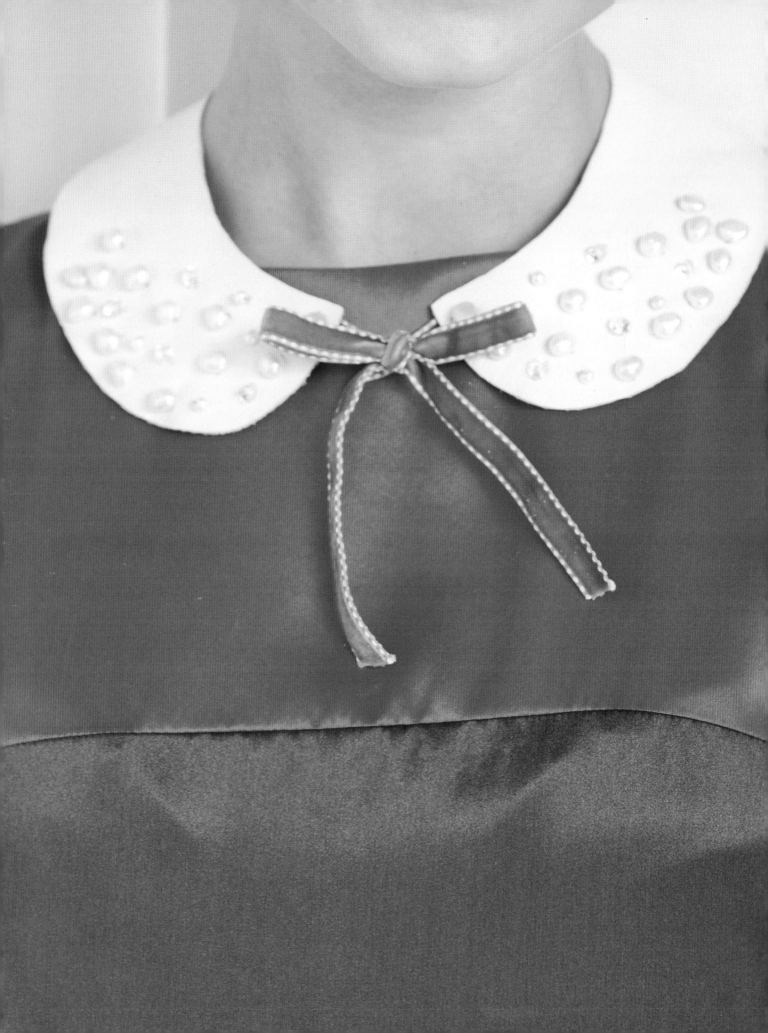

Peter Pan collar

Use a piece of leather and a velvet ribbon to create this versatile collar. Bead the entire collar for a real luxury look, or try using felt instead of leather and sew the beads straight onto the felt.

Materials

- Pencil and paper
- Pins
- Scrap fabric
- Leather
- Selection of beads
- Velvet ribbon
- Beading needle and thread
- Scissors
- Sticky tape
- Spatula and latex adhesive
- Parchment paper
- Leather punch

1 Draw the pattern for your collar on paper, cut this out and use it as a test pattern on scrap fabric. Fold the fabric in half, pin in place and cut out. Check that the fabric collar fits and sits comfortably and make adjustments to the pattern before cutting the leather. Fold the leather in half, and secure in place with some sticky tape.

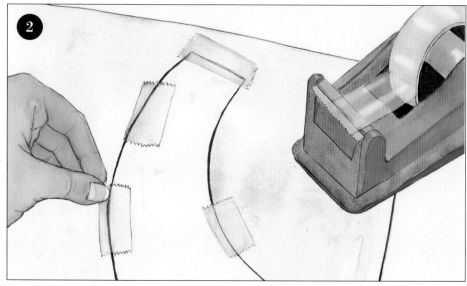

2 Attach the pattern to the leather using sticky tape. Position the pattern so that one of its ends is flush with the fold.

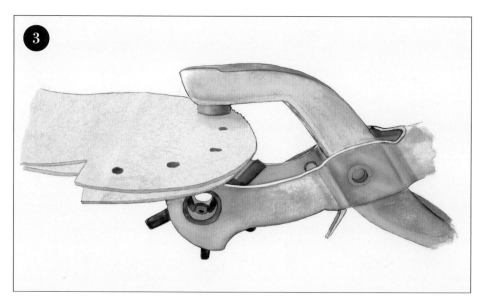

3 Using a sharp, sturdy pair of scissors cut around the pattern as neatly as possible; any rough edges can be trimmed later. Use more tape to keep the pattern stuck in the fold. Take a leather punch, and make a number of punches in the collar. Try to space them so there will be gaps between the beads.

Collar Template

Photocopy at 144%

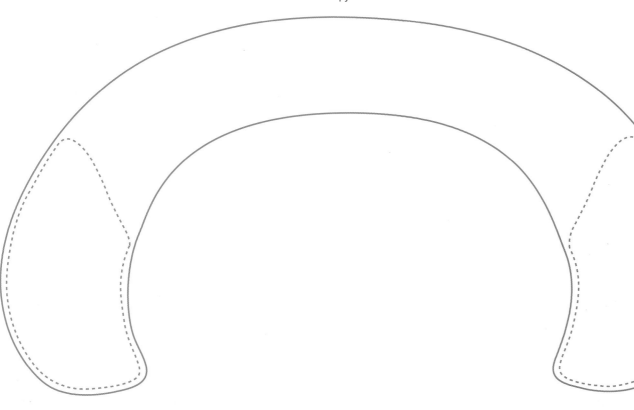

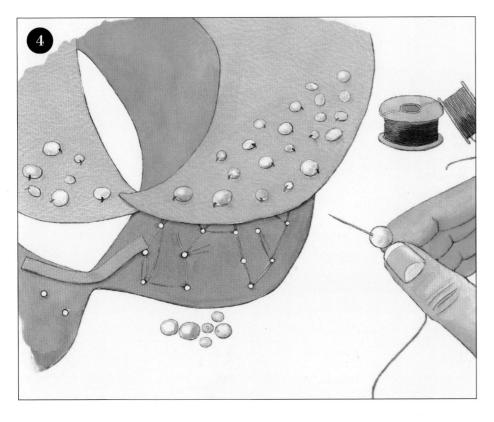

4   Thread a beading needle with suitable thread and start to sew the beads onto the leather collar. Sew the first bead, keeping hold of the end of the thread, add the second and third beads, and then sew back through them to the first; tie off the loose thread. Add all further beads in the same way. Take two lengths of velvet ribbon and sew one to each side of the collar as a tie, to secure the collar in place. Use a spatula to add a thin layer of latex adhesive (or suitable craft glue) to stick cutouts of leather onto the back of the collar; this will hide the stitching threads on the back of the collar, secure the beads, and make it comfortable to wear.

Suede and silver necklace

––––––––––

Use basic metalwork tools and skills to create this beautiful necklace, which is simply embellished by silver tubes made from silver sheet with individually textured surfaces. Make a matching bracelet using shorter lengths of suede.

Materials

- ⅝in x 2½in (15mm x 60mm) of 0.7mm Sterling silver sheet
- ⅜in x 2in (10mm x 50mm) of 0.7mm Sterling silver sheet (for bracelet)
- US 14 gauge (SWG 16, 15mm) Sterling silver round wire
- Microfiber suede
- Findings selection (see page 10)
- Beading thread
- Superglue or epoxy resin
- Scissors
- Hammers
- Two pair of pliers
- Steel block
- Rawhide or nylon mallet
- Center punch
- Drill
- Round file
- Pipe or mandrel
- Tape measure or ruler

Tips

Oxidize the silver with liver of sulfur, to really show the texture.

Try using copper for an alternative finish.

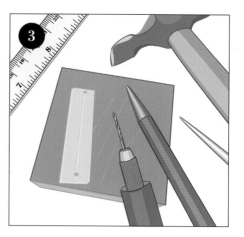

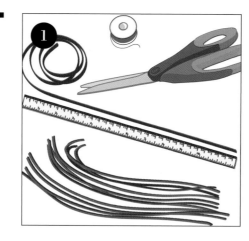

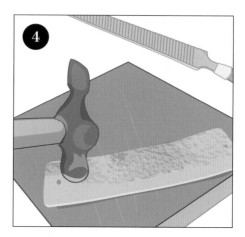

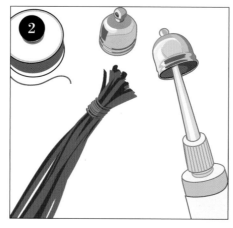

1 Measure and cut twelve 18in (46cm) lengths of microfiber suede. Gather all lengths together and use beading thread to whip the ends together. Do this by wrapping the thread tightly around all of the strands, secure with a couple of knots and a dab of glue. Snip away excess ends.

2 Add suitable glue to the inside of an end cap: superglue or epoxy resin will work well. Push the whipped end into the end cap and hold in place for a few seconds. Depending on the glue used, place to one side to allow to dry fully. Repeat on the other end once the silver tubes have been added.

3 Use a ruler to find the center point of the silver sheet, marking out a point on either end where a hole will be made. Place the silver onto a steel block and then use a center punch and hammer to create the guide hole. Use a drill and round file to complete the hole in the silver: this needs to be able to accommodate the silver wire.

4 Use a suitable file to round off each of the corners of the silver sheet. Then place back onto a steel block, and use your chosen hammer to create an even texture over the surface of the sheet. Start at one end and work your way back and forth using an even strike, taking care along the edges.

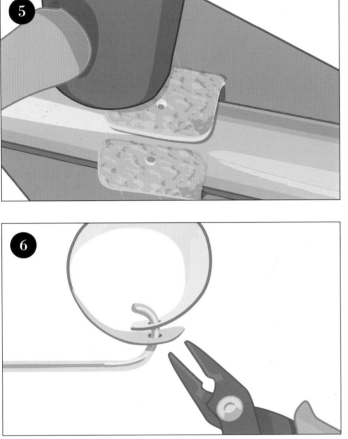

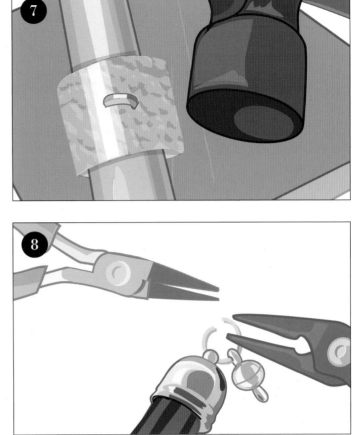

5 Use a metal cylinder, a cut-off section of pipe, or if you have one, a mandrel. Use fingers to begin to bend the silver around the cylinder. Use a rawhide or nylon mallet to ensure the silver forms a neat tube shape, and that the two holes are lined up, ready for the next step.

6 Thread a length of round wire through the two holes and then use pliers to create a bend in the wire on the inside of the silver tube. Use a pair of wire cutters to trim the wire, leaving approximately ³⁄₁₆in (5mm) on the outside of the silver tube. Use a file to neaten the end of the wire.

7 Place the silver tube back onto the pipe or mandrel, and then use a hammer to flatten the wire on both sides of the silver tube. Take care to strike the wire only, so you don't lose the texture pattern on the tube. Use a polishing cloth to rub over the whole tube, producing a lovely shine.

8 Create two more silver tubes for the necklace and a smaller one to use to create a matching bracelet. Thread all three tubes onto the microfiber suede from the previous steps, and then repeat Step 2. Use two pairs of pliers to open a jumpring to add a suitable clasp to both ends of the necklace (see page 12).

Resources

UK

Bead Aura
114 Colindale Avenue
London
NW9 5GX
Tel: +44 (0)744 075 7208
www.beadaura.co.uk

The Bead Merchant
22 Observer way
Kelvedon
Essex
CO5 9NZ
Tel: +44 (0)1376 570022
www.beadmerchant.co.uk

The Bead Shop
44 Higher Ardwick
Manchester
M12 6DA
Tel: +44 (0)161 274 4040
www.the-beadshop.co.uk

Beads Direct
10 Duke Street
Loughborough
Leicestershire
LE11 1ED
Tel: +44 (0)1509 218028
www.beadsdirect.co.uk

Beadsisters
Mid Cairngarroch Croft
Stoneykirk
Stranraer
Wigtownshire
DG9 9EH
Tel: +44 (0)1776 830352
www.beadsisters.co.uk

Bijoux Beads
Elton House
2 Abbey Street
Bath
BA1 1NN
Tel: +44 (0)1225 482024
www.bijouxbeads.co.uk

Cookson Gold
59-83 Vittoria Street
Birmingham
B1 3NZ
Tel: +44 (0)345 100 1122
www.cooksongold.com

Fred Aldous
37 Lever Street
Manchester
M1 1LW
Tel: +44 (0)161 236 4224
www.fredaldous.co.uk

The Genuine Gemstone Company
Unit 2D Eagle Road
Moons Moat
Redditch
Worcestershire
B98 9HF
Tel: +44 (0)1527 406100
www.tggc.com

GJ Beads
Unit L
St Erth Industrial Estate
Hayle
Cornwall
TR27 6LP
Tel: +44 (0)1736 751070
www.gjbeads.co.uk

Jillybeads
1 Anstable Road
Morecambe
LA4 6TG
Tel: +44 (0)1524 412728
www.jillybeads.co.uk

Palmer Metals
401 Broad Lane
Coventry
CV5 7AY
Tel: +44 (0)845 644 9343
www.palmermetals.co.uk

Spoilt Rotten Beads
7 The Green
Haddenham
Ely
Cambridgeshire
CB6 3TA
Tel: +44 (0)1353 749853
www.spoiltrottenbeads.co.uk

Wires.co.uk
Unit 3 Zone A
Chelmsford Road Industrial
Estate
Great Dunmow
Essex
CM6 1HD
Tel: +44 (0)1371 238013
https://wires.co.uk

USA

Fire Mountain Gems and Beads
1 Fire Mountain Way
Grants Pass
OR 97526-2373
Tel: +1 800 355 2137
(toll free)
Tel: +1 541 956 7890
www.firemountaingems.com

Vintaj Natural Brass Company
5140 US 20 W
Galena, Il 61036
www.vintaj.com

AUSTRALIA

Beads Online
Tel: +61 (0)2 6674 4570
www.beadsonline.com.au

Over the Rainbow
PO Box 9112
Seaford
Victoria 3198
Tel: +61 (0)3 9785 3800
www.polymerclay.com.au

Online
www.bettsmetals.com
www.docrafts.com
www.i-beads.co.uk
www.knottingways.co.uk
www.leprevo.co.uk
www.prettypebblesbeads.co.uk
www.resin8co.uk
www.robins-beads.co.uk

Index

To place an order, or to request a catalogue, contact:

GMC Publications Ltd

Castle Place, 166 High Street, Lewes, East Sussex, BN7 1XU

United Kingdom

Tel: +44 (0)1273 488005

www.gmcbooks.com